MommaEarth Goddess Runes

Also by Kim Antieau

Old Mermaids Books
The Blue Tail • Church of the Old Mermaids • The First Book of Old Mermaids Tales • The Fish Wife • An Old Mermaid Journal • The Old Mermaids Book of Days and Nights • The Old Mermaids Book of Days and Nights: A Year and a Day Journal • The Second Book of Old Mermaids Tales

Other Novels
Broken Moon • Butch • Coyote Cowgirl • Deathmark • The Desert Siren • Her Frozen Wild • The Gaia Websters • Jewelweed Station • The Jigsaw Woman • Maternal Instincts • Mercy, Unbound • The Monster's Daughter • Queendom: Feast of the Saints • The Rift • Ruby's Imagine • Swans in Winter • Whackadoodle Times • Whackadoodle Times Two

Other Nonfiction
Answering the Creative Call • Certified: Learning to Repair Myself and the World in the Emerald City • Counting on Wildflowers: An Entanglement • The Salmon Mysteries: a Reimagining of the Eleusinian Mysteries • The Salmon Mysteries Workbook: Reimagining the Eleusinian Mysteries • The Old Mermaids Oracle • Under the Tucson Moon

Other Collections
Entangled Realities (with Mario Milosevic) *• Fun with Vic and Jane • Haunted • Tales Fabulous and Fairy • Trudging to Eden*

Chapbook
Blossoms

Blog
www.kimantieau.com

Photography
www.kimantieau.smugmug.com

MommaEarth Goddess Runes

Kim Antieau

Green Snake
PUBLISHING

MommaEarth Goddess Runes
by Kim Antieau

Copyright © 2018 by Kim Antieau.

ISBN: 978-1-949644-42-5

All rights reserved.

www.kimantieau.com

No part of this book may be reproduced without written permission of the author.

Cover photo by Kim Antieau.
Book design by Mario Milosevic.

Published by Green Snake Publishing.

www.greensnakepublishing.com

Contents

Introduction 7

How to use MEGR 11

⚵ Athene 17

Brigid 21

⚳ Ceres 25

Eriskegal 29

⚷ Hekate 33

Inanna 37

Isis 41

Kali 45

Kuan Yin 49

Nyx 53

Spider Woman 57

⚶ Vesta 61

☾ Yemaya 65

Introduction

I originally created a set of six MommaEarth Goddess Runes for a friend's croning in 1993. After I gave her the gift, I could not stop thinking about the Goddess Runes. I wanted a set for myself!

For this new set, I chose 13 Goddesses because the number 13 is such a sacred number for women. Far from being unlucky, this number represents the 13 moons of the year. I picked Goddesses from various cultures. Most have been diminished and dismembered by patriarchal storytelling. With the creation of these MommaEarth Goddess Runes (MEGR), I hope to help us re-member them truly, unhampered by fear or oppression.

I initially looked for Goddesses who had simple

symbols which I could easily render onto stone. However, the MEGR had a life of their own. Certain Goddesses wanted to be included, but I could not find appropriate simple symbols. One night I dreamed several of the symbols. The next morning I sat down and completed the design and text.

These are obviously not Nordic runes. I use the word "runes" in its Old English meaning: a secret, a mystery. Although I have written here what you might expect each MEGR to mean, the true secrets and mysteries of the Goddesses will be revealed to you the more you use them.

If you don't have a set of the runes made by me, you can easily make your own set for your own use. (They are my intellectual property, so you cannot sell sets of them.) You can paint the symbols on rocks, gems, shells, or pieces of wood. You could also make a set of cards with the symbol on each card. Use your imagination and creativity.

When you first have your set of MEGR, I suggest that you pick out one a day for 13 days. Spend a day with whichever Goddess you choose that day. See what the day is like and what dreams you have the night before or the night after. Take notes. After you have used MEGR for a while, you might even want to research each Goddess.

If you don't have a set of MEGR yet, you can still do a Goddess a day. Just flip through this book until you land on one.

Enjoy yourself!

Love,

Kim Antieau

P.S. If you want me to create a set for you, you can email me at kim@kimantieau.com for prices. But I promise you: You can easily make your own!

How to use the MommaEarth Goddess Runes

Single Rune Reading

Find a quiet place or a quiet moment. Close your eyes and breathe deeply. Think about your day or any issues you wish to explore. Reach into the bag and pull out the first MommaEarth Goddess Rune you touch. Look up the symbol in your booklet and allow the Goddess to speak to you. If the reading doesn't seem to fit, carry the stone (or whatever the symbol is on) with you throughout the day. At the end of the day look at the stone and read about the corresponding Goddess again. Now see what you are able to intuit.

Triple Goddess Reading

Find a quiet place. Close your eyes and breathe deeply. Think about your past, present, and future and any issues you wish to explore. Pull out three MEGR, one at a time.

The first MEGR represents your Maiden Aspect (or your past). The second MEGR represents your Mother Aspect (or your present). The third MEGR represents your Crone Aspect (or your future).

Maiden	Mother	Crone
O	O	O
Past	Present	Future

These three aspects signify the stages a woman goes through during her life, her monthly cycle, and sometimes her daily cycle!

The Maiden Aspect is the part of you that

is newly formed, beginning, adventurous, impulsive, childish and childlike. The first MommaEarth Goddess Rune you chose in this reading influences your past and your Maiden aspects. Think of her and She will help you see more clearly how your past and present child-self are influencing your present day.

The Mother Aspect is the part of you who is the source of all, the one who bleeds once a month and does not die. This is the part of you who births, rebirths, heals, and creates. She represents the middle of the cycle of Maiden, Mother, Crone. Meditate on her, and She will help you feel your power as a Creatrix in the present.

Crone is the final aspect of the triple goddess. She is the part of you who knows all, the one who can find the answer always within the universe of knowledge that is yourself. She is the part of you who understands transformation, death, and ending. She is your fairy Goddessmother who can grant your every wish. Meditate on her, and you will come to understand your past, present, and future. She will help you see your place in the universe.

Sacred Life Reading

Trying to balance work and home and live a sacred life is one of the more difficult challenges of modern life.

When you're feeling you cannot balance home and work or you just need help doing so, close your eyes and think about home and work. Then draw out three stones.

The first Goddess will help you at home, the second Goddess will help you remember your sacred life at work, and the third Goddess will help you balance both.

Meditate on all three and you will find the answers you need about work and home.

Healing the Mind-Body Split

Imagine it: a time when our mind and body were one, when nature was revered instead of reviled, when the Goddess in all things was honored, when logic and intuition guided us toward truth. By healing the split—bridging the chasm between body and mind—I believe we can heal ourselves of many of the physical and emotional illnesses that plague our lives.

Close your eyes, breathe deeply, and pull out three stones. As always, take out the first stones you actually touch.

The first stone represents the Goddess who presently influences your mind.

The second stone will reveal the Goddess who presently influences your body. Both these Goddesses protect and guide you on your journey.

The third MEGR reveals the Goddess who will help you heal the split between your mind and body. She will assist you in bringing together the aspects of the Goddesses who influence your body and mind. She is your special healer.

Meditate on her, dream of her, write about her in your journal or on the notes pages in this booklet. She will help you re-member the time before you were split, the time when you were whole.

And so . . .

As you use the MommaEarth Goddess Runes, you will create your own layouts, and you will discover personal insights and meanings for the Goddesses which pertain especially to you.

This is part of the wonderful magical mystery tour the MommaEarth Goddess Runes will take you on.

Athene

Healing and self-hood

This ancient Minoan Goddess of healing, purification, and alchemy is a virgin: one-in-herself. She represents female self-determination and skill in the arts. When you choose Athene, She will help you stand firm in yourself and be an alchemist: changing lead to gold in all aspects of your life. Call upon her to help in healing and transformations of all kinds.

Notes

Brigid

Inspiration and healing

The Celtic Triple Goddess of Fire, Brigid gives the gifts of inspiration, smithcraft, and healing. She teaches us how to mourn and whistle for our friends. When you call upon Brigid, She will help you heal by teaching you to open yourself to your artistic gifts. Whether you are gardening, creating a poem, or singing in the shower, Brigid will help you breathe and feel your fire. Don't forget to whistle for your friends when you're feeling alone and uninspired. They are aspects of the Goddess, too.

Notes

Ceres

Good Harvest and a Just World

Ceres is the Great Goddess, Mother of the Harvest, the source of food and justice. When you call upon Ceres, you are calling upon the Great Mother of the Harvest and the Justice system. She will help you find justice, and She will help you be a just lawgiver. Always, She will help you find the nurturing and nutrition you need from the world.

Notes

Eriskegal

Truth

Great Sumerian Goddess of the Underworld, Eriskegal rules the underworld while her sister, Inanna, rules the Heavens and the Earth. Eriskegal is who you call upon when you fall into depression. She will gnash her teeth, tear out her hair, and scream at you until you are ready to face your truths. In the belly of the great Earth Mother, you can see yourself for who you really are. Tear down the facades of the outer world. Sometimes it is good to feel sorry for yourself. Do not fear depression or stay too long in it.

Notes

Hekate

Crossroads

As the Egyptian Triple Goddess of midwifery, wiseblood, and regeneration, Hekate is maiden, mother, and crone. She is Queen of the Witches, Goddess of the crossroads. She will help midwife a child, an idea, or your true self. She will meet you alone at the crossroads and help you decide which path to take.

Notes

Inanna

Courage

Inanna is the Sumerian Goddess of the Heavens and the Earth who brings agriculture, arts, and law to her people. She has everything, yet She heeds the call of the underworld. She faces the wrath of her sister Eriskegal, dies, and is reborn. When you call upon Inanna, She will give you the courage to take the journey to the underworld, go places where family and friends desert you, and find the place deep inside yourself that you fear the most. She will help you accept that you will never be the same after the journey.

Notes

Isis

Resurrection

Great Goddess of Egypt, Mother of All, Isis brings forth herself. She is the Goddess from whom all arise. She is Bright Mother/Dark Mother, representing birth/death/rebirth. She teaches women how to grind corn, make cloth, and tame men. When you call upon Isis, She will help you live in the world of men. When you feel dis-membered, She will help you re-member and be true to yourself.

Notes

Kali

Awakening

Indian Goddess of Life and Destruction, Kali is the Dark Mother. She is called into being when life is out of balance. She will stand alone and destroy that which must fall. She is the womb and the tomb. The Primal Deep. She destroys and then sleeps and new ages arise from her. When you call upon Kali, you are ready for the great awakening. Structures and ideas will shatter. She will help you create, preserve, and destroy.

Notes

Kuan Yin

Compassion and Faith

Chinese Goddess of Compassion, Mercy, and Peace, Kuan Yin chooses to keep her human form and remain on Earth until all living creatures attain enlightenment. Her name means "She who hears the weeping world." She is salvation from physical and spiritual harm. Call her name, and you will be healed. Whisper her name again, and you will be rescued. Kuan Yin helps you remember that you are never alone; She cares for you and will help keep you from harm.

Notes

Nyx

Mother-right

Ancient Goddess of Night, daughter of Chaos, mother of the Furies and Fates, Nyx is the ultimate mother, the one who births the Cosmic Egg. She is the dark feminine principle. She is night, and She births light and gives us the ability to see beyond the present. When you call upon Nyx, She will help you mother all your creations, including yourself. She will help you see beyond the night to create the future you desire.

Notes

Spider Woman

Connectedness

Earth Goddess of the Native people of the Southwestern United States, Spider Woman is Creator of All. When She creates us, She attaches a thread from her web to our heads so we will always remember that we are connected to her. When we forget, we close the door to her wisdom and our own knowingness. Call upon Spider Woman when you have forgotten your connectedness to all things. By chanting, you will open yourself to the Goddess and link yourself to the creative wisdom once again.

Notes

Vesta

At Home With Yourself

Vesta is the guardian of innermost things. Her altar is the center of the Earth. From her hearth, all things come: food, wisdom, storytelling, herstory. All. When you call upon Vesta, She will help you find your deepest darkest self, walk through dark places, and cherish times of darkness as nourishment for the soul. Through her, you will find the divine and sacred in every commonplace task you undertake.

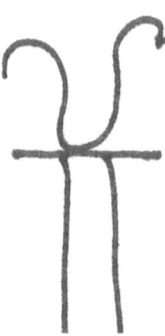

Notes

Yemaya

Intuition

African Goddess of the Ocean and Moon, Yemaya reminds us to use our gift of intuition. She teaches us how to live and be aware of the phases of the Moon and our bodies. She reminds us to take time for reflection and honor our connection to all women. Call upon Yemaya when you need to learn how to live in this world with sacredness. She will help you listen to your waking and sleeping dreams.

Notes

www.ingramcontent.com/pod-product-compliance
Lightning Source LLC
Chambersburg PA
CBHW030104100526
44591CB00008B/259